JOANNA MURRAY-SMITH

Joanna Murray-Smith's plays have been produced in many languages, all over the world, including on the West End, Broadway and at the Royal National Theatre. Her plays include *American Song*, *Pennsylvania Avenue*, *Fury*, *Songs for Nobodies*, *True Minds*, *Day One – A Hotel – Evening*, *The Gift*, *Rockabye*, *The Female of the Species*, *Ninety*, *Bombshells*, *Rapture*, *Nightfall*, *Redemption*, *Flame*, *Love Child*, *Atlanta*, *Honour*, *Angry Young Penguins* and two upcoming plays, *Berlin* and *L'Appartement*. She has also adapted *Hedda Gabler*, as well as Ingmar Bergman's *Scenes from a Marriage*, for Sir Trevor Nunn (London). Her three novels (published by Penguin/Viking) are *Truce*, *Judgement Rock* and *Sunnyside*. Her opera libretti include *Love in the Age of Therapy* and *The Divorce*. Joanna has also written many screenplays.

Joanna Murray-Smith

SWITZERLAND

NICK HERN BOOKS

London

www.nickhernbooks.co.uk

A Nick Hern Book

Switzerland first published in Great Britain as a paperback original in 2018 by Nick Hern Books Limited, The Glasshouse, 49a Goldhawk Road, London W12 8QP by arrangement with Currency Press Pty Ltd, PO Box 2287, Strawberry Hills, NSW 2012, Australia, www.currency.com.au

Switzerland copyright © 2016, 2018 Joanna Murray-Smith

Joanna Murray-Smith has asserted her right to be identified as the author of this work

Cover design by Bob King Creative
Back cover photograph (Calum Finlay and Phyllis Logan in the 2018 UK premiere) by Nobby Clark

Designed and typeset by Nick Hern Books
Printed in the UK by Mimeo Ltd, Huntingdon, Cambridgeshire PE29 6XX

A CIP catalogue record for this book is available from the British Library

ISBN   978 1 84842 821 8

Woodland
CARBON
www.woodlandcarbon.co.uk
NICK HERN BOOKS
Printed on Carbon Captured paper

The co-world premiere of *Switzerland* was first presented, by special arrangement with the Geffen Playhouse, by Sydney Theatre Company at the Drama Theatre, Sydney Opera House on 3 November 2014, with the following cast:

PATRICIA HIGHSMITH	Sarah Peirse
EDWARD	Eamon Farren

Director	Sarah Goodes
Production Designer	Michael Scott-Mitchell
Lighting Designer	Nick Schlieper
Composer & Sound Designer	Steve Francis
Voice and Text Coach	Charmian Gradwell
Wardrobe and Wigs	David Jennings

The play was commissioned and presented as a co-world premiere by the Geffen Playhouse at the Audrey Skirball Kenis Theater, Los Angeles, on 6 March 2015, with the following cast:

PATRICIA HIGHSMITH	Laura Linney
EDWARD	Seth Numrich

Director	Mark Brokaw
Scenic Designer	Anthony T. Fanning
Costume Designer	Ellen McCartney
Lighting Designer	Lap Chi Chu
Composer & Sound Designer	John Ballinger

The play received its European premiere, produced by Theatre Royal Bath Productions and Jonathan Church Productions, at the Ustinov Studio, Theatre Royal Bath, on 9 August 2018, with the following cast:

PATRICIA HIGHSMITH   Phyllis Logan
EDWARD   Calum Finlay

Director   Lucy Bailey
Designer   William Dudley
Lighting Designer   Chris Davey
Sound Designer   Mic Pool
Casting Director   Ginny Schiller CDG
Assistant Director   Clemmie Reynolds

The production transferred to the Ambassadors Theatre, London, on 10 November 2018.

Acknowledgements

I would like to express my gratitude to Randall Arney, Amy Levinson, the late Gil Cates and the staff of the Geffen Playhouse, to Andrew Upton and the staff of the Sydney Theatre Company, to Sarah Goodes and Mark Brokaw and to the brilliant cast members of both the Sydney and Los Angeles productions: Sarah Peirse, Eamon Farren, Laura Linney and Seth Numrich.

I would also like to thank the team behind the first British production, particularly Lucy Bailey, Clemmie Reynolds, Phyllis Logan and Calum Finlay, who so diligently and inspiringly took on the challenges of a still-evolving play.

Switzerland was written whilst I was a Vice-Chancellor's Fellow at the University of Melbourne. I would like to thank Professor Glyn Davis and the university for this inspiring experience.

The very much missed Sarah Jane Leigh was instrumental in the writing of this play.

Love and thanks, as always, to Raymond Gill.

J.M-S.

For Nita Murray-Smith

Characters:

PATRICIA HIGHSMITH, *an older woman, distinct vestiges
of beauty*

EDWARD, *twenties, handsome, sexually ambiguous,
a New Yorker*

Setting

*It's 1995. We are in the spacious study of Patricia Highsmith, in
her minimalist modern house in Tegna, Switzerland. By contrast
to the bunker-like architecture, the study is a brilliant archive of
a life. Books, pictures, rugs and artefacts – all somehow unique
or beautiful – fill the space, including a collection of antique
weapons, both knives and guns. The overall effect is curatorial
rather than cluttered. Her desk is furnished with a 1956
Olympia Deluxe typewriter, papers, an ashtray, a packet of
Camel cigarettes – she smokes on and off throughout the play –
a half-empty bottle of Scotch and a glass. Through the window,
is a classic picture-postcard vista of Switzerland.*

*This text went to press before the end of rehearsals and so may
differ slightly from the play as performed.*

ACT ONE

Lights up. 1995. Autumn. Early morning. PATRICIA
HIGHSMITH *is sitting at her desk. She is wearing men's
trousers, a boy's shirt and loafers. She is older now, but there
are vestiges of her once-great beauty and she has an innate
gender-neutral style.* EDWARD, *an ordinarily handsome young
man of around twenty-five – neatly if inexpensively dressed – is
standing. A backpack and a small suitcase sit beside him on the
floor. His demeanour is distinctly nervous. He's been dreaming
of this moment and it's finally arrived.*

PATRICIA (*without turning to look at him, still typing*). You're
late.

EDWARD. Oh.

PATRICIA. I know that because this is Switzerland.

Beat. She turns around to take him in.

EDWARD. The train was um… late leaving Paris.

PATRICIA. Is that my business?

EDWARD. I tried to call from the *Gare du Nord* –

PATRICIA. I don't answer the phone.

EDWARD. I did email to say –

PATRICIA. I don't do email.

EDWARD. No, I get that –

PATRICIA. – if you're impulsive, it's downright dangerous.

EDWARD. I guess that's true!

PATRICIA. No one realises that the whole point of an envelope
and a stamp is to act as a buffer between *thought* and *deed*.
I can sound very pleasant, benevolent even, in a letter, but in an
email, my personal generosity doesn't come through. I emailed
my German publisher and he completely misread my tone.

EDWARD. What did you write?

PATRICIA. I said '*What the hell makes you think I'm going to have the goddamn wool pulled over my eyes by a bunch of Nazis who'd sell their mother to make an extra Deutschmark?*'… It came across as 'hostile' apparently.

He steps forward nervously and offers his hand.

EDWARD. Edward Ridgeway.

She looks at it disdainfully. He retracts it.

Miss Highsmith, I'm hoping we're going to address the situation –

PATRICIA. The 'situation' –

EDWARD. I think we both know –

PATRICIA. I guess we do know –

EDWARD. The reason I'm here –

PATRICIA. You're the troubleshooter?

EDWARD. Well, I'm confident that –

PATRICIA. Confident, eh? Think you're going to 'sort me out'?

EDWARD. Well –

PATRICIA. Once upon a time, you could *depend* upon confidence. People asked themselves: Do I have the *right* to be confident? You *earned* that degree of self-affirmation.

EDWARD. Well, I –

PATRICIA. Whereas these days, young people… they *start out* confident. Why? I'll tell you why! Because they're deluded. They're *silly little fuckers*! And then *life* has to take the wind out of their sails.

EDWARD. I don't think I'm deluded!

PATRICIA. That's because you *are* deluded, genius!

EDWARD. Miss Highsmith, first of all I want to take this opportunity to say that we're sure it was just all some kind of misunderstanding.

PATRICIA. Who's 'we'?

EDWARD. Mr Hunter and the company. And I would certainly add my vote to that.

PATRICIA. You would, would you? Are you old enough to vote?

EDWARD (*carefully*). We think Bradley Applebee probably just allowed himself to let his imagination get the better of him.

PATRICIA. Bradley Applebee didn't have any imagination.

EDWARD. Well, his mind –

PATRICIA. There was no indication Applebee had a mind, either.

EDWARD. The company wants you to know there are no hard feelings.

PATRICIA. Presumably, Applebee has a couple of hard feelings.

EDWARD. Well, actually he's –

PATRICIA. What?

EDWARD. Bradley's left the company.

Beat.

PATRICIA. Well, no doubt this is all some distant memory for Bradley Applebee. He's probably pushing a pen in some mediocre office as we speak.

EDWARD. Oh no – no, Bradley's not ready for work yet.

PATRICIA. 'Not ready'?

EDWARD. Well, he's – ah – in counselling. I think he took it rather hard.

PATRICIA. The company had no business sending a timid little nobody with no sense of humour.

EDWARD. He's still having flashbacks, apparently –

PATRICIA. Flashbacks!

EDWARD. About the knife.

PATRICIA. There was no knife!

EDWARD. Well, that's what we mean about his imagination taking the lead.

PATRICIA. As if I'd –

EDWARD. Exactly. That's what we said. As if Miss Highsmith would –

PATRICIA. I don't have time to threaten underlings with –

EDWARD. Of course not!

PATRICIA. I'm not in the habit of –

EDWARD. He kept saying it wouldn't have been so bad in the daylight –

PATRICIA. *Nothing's* so bad in the daylight. That's why we revel in darkness!

EDWARD. For whatever reason, he had a strong sense of waking up in the pitch black and feeling the steel blade against his throat –

PATRICIA. Crazy.

EDWARD. Crazy. Exactly.

PATRICIA. *He* woke *me* up in the dead of night. It's not my fault Hunter sent a kid with a capacity to hallucinate. I tell you what though, that kid could scream! Hitchcock would have bottled it.

EDWARD. Anyhow, Bradley aside, we still feel very strongly –

PATRICIA. 'We'?

EDWARD. Mr Hunter and the company –

PATRICIA. Want to make some money.

EDWARD. Well, yes. Okay. Companies generally like to make money. Is there anything wrong with that?

PATRICIA. They want to make money off of me.

EDWARD. They want *you* to make money, too.

PATRICIA. I'm touched.

EDWARD. And they wanted me to come and tell you that the reason they are overlooking – the reason I'm here, is to let you know we have every confidence.

PATRICIA. Really? You're the company spokesman? You've still got your baby teeth!

EDWARD. I'm older than I look. And not to blow my own trumpet but I think I have the sensibility to understand you.

PATRICIA. Notice how it's only trumpet-blowers who use that phrase?

EDWARD. I think I can help and everyone will be happy.

PATRICIA. From the moment you walked through that door, I could see that you brought all the slapdash of America with you. Maybe I've been in Europe too long, but the attention to detail is very beguiling here – Europeans use their *senses*. Americans like you and Americans *are* like you, think close enough is good enough. It's a general national callow youth. The sensibility is just not *fine*. How is your mind? Is it a fine mind?

EDWARD. My mind?

PATRICIA. Is the taxi still here? Tell him to keep the meter on.

EDWARD. Please, Miss Highsmith –

PATRICIA. That's the very best thing about Switzerland. When you call a cab, *the cab comes*.

EDWARD. Just give me a chance – just a –

PATRICIA. They should put *that* on the tourism ads. Enough with the *chocolate*, for Christ's sake.

EDWARD. I've come a long way.

PATRICIA. Yes, you have. And for absolutely no reason.

EDWARD. All the way from New York City.

PATRICIA. New York City!

EDWARD. The greatest city on earth.

PATRICIA. The greatest city on earth! Full of pseuds and Jews and Catholics! *The greatest city?* Is that where you get your air of self-congratulation? Sitting there at your little desk in a publishing house that thinks it's hit the big time with Tom Wolfe. Tom Wolfe! What a joke! I can see you in your cheap suit sitting in Emmett's coffee shop thinking that those pretty girls eating pie and drinking coffee are going to be impressed that you're some big cheese because you get to fraternise with authors. Like you're an intellectual!

EDWARD. Emmett's has gone.

PATRICIA. What?

EDWARD. There is no Emmett's.

PATRICIA (*wind out of sails*). Emmett's is gone?

EDWARD. And girls don't eat pie. They eat… *Romaine*.

PATRICIA. What the hell is Romaine?

EDWARD. It's a lettuce. They eat lettuce. And yogurt. There are very few – (*Makes the quotation mark sign with his fingers.*) 'diners'.

PATRICIA (*mimicking and nasty*). Please don't do that.

EDWARD (*continuing*). And girls don't smoke.

PATRICIA. They don't smoke?

EDWARD. Nobody smokes. Apart from models.

PATRICIA. Nobody smokes?

EDWARD. And they don't drink coffee – they get organic caffè lattes in paper cups to go.

PATRICIA. What the hell is *that*?

EDWARD. It's the new coffee.

PATRICIA. I liked the old coffee! Caffè lattes! So Americans can pretend they're in Europe even though they don't know where it is!

EDWARD. There are also nineteen different brands of bottled water –

PATRICIA. What happened to *tap* water?

EDWARD. That's like saying what happened to white bread.

PATRICIA. What happened to white bread?

EDWARD. We lost the fight.

PATRICIA. Who lost the fight?

EDWARD. White-bread lovers of the world. It's all rice cakes and oat loaves. Don't even mention butter.

PATRICIA. Good God!

EDWARD. A little African ceramic dish of Ligurian virgin olive oil, perhaps. But butter, Jesus, keep your voice down!

PATRICIA. And if you don't happen to have any Ligurian virgins on hand?

EDWARD. You couldn't possibly have a character who eats a Wonder Bread sandwich any more. White-bread eating is an act of a dedicated radicalised anarchist. Which, of course, is someone you *could* write!

PATRICIA. Maybe this country has influenced me, but there's altogether too much *personality* going on here: you and your world view about what I can and can't do. I don't know why I said yes to Hunter. He manipulated me, that fucker! He said: 'I'm sending an emissary to persuade you to sign and by the way he can bring you over some of the things you want' and I fell for it. He didn't tell me the emissary would be *twelve years old. Goodbye.*

EDWARD. You don't mean that.

PATRICIA. I mean it. And I'm not signing a damn thing.

A momentary steeliness comes over the genial EDWARD.

EDWARD. *Yes, you will.*

Beat.

PATRICIA (*stunned*). I beg your pardon?

EDWARD. You will sign. In the end.

PATRICIA. Get lost. Get outta here. Before I call the cops. Who won't like you. 'Cause they don't like trouble. That's why they're neutral. Trouble bothers them. I'll say you're an intruder and they'll haul your ass into a Swiss jail where they'll torture you with intravenous bircher muesli!

She holds his gaze. Beat. He gets up, walks to the door. Stops. The steeliness is gone.

EDWARD. I'm not going until I say what I came to say.

She's surprised at his gumption.

First of all, I volunteered for this.

PATRICIA. You think that impresses me?

EDWARD (*summoning the courage*). Because I *get* you.

PATRICIA. Oh! You 'get' me! You impertinent little –

EDWARD (*battling on*). From the first time I read *Strangers on a Train*, I felt something. I felt a connection.

PATRICIA. Yeah, well funny, but *I didn't*! A connection joins two things. You're one thing. And I'm the other and I don't feel any connection. *Goodbye.*

EDWARD (*not fawning*). *Nobody* writes the way you do. As Graham Greene said: 'The poet of apprehension.' *You are a brilliant writer.*

PATRICIA. You and Graham Greene! He'd be so touched and I can die happy!

EDWARD. I've always wished that I could write like you –

PATRICIA. Jesus H. Christ! If you want to write: *write*. Don't ask *me* for permission. The world is full of people who should be actively *discouraged* from taking pen to paper. Discouraged as in *forcibly restrained*, if necessary. Or even physically assaulted. Whatever it takes!

EDWARD. Oh, I could never write but I think I have a little insight into real writers.

PATRICIA. *Oh, really?*

EDWARD. The writers we represent at the company… Great writers who have changed the face –

PATRICIA. *Great* writers!

EDWARD. Well, *yes*. Yes. Great writers. Yes. (*An element of knowing, here*.) Like Vonnegut –

PATRICIA. Vonnegut! My God!

EDWARD. You don't like – you don't – ?

PATRICIA (*incredulous*). *Vonnegut?*

EDWARD. *The New York Times Book Review*: 'A towering force in twentieth-century literature – there may be no greater claimant to acute satirical observation.'

PATRICIA (*furious*). There's a point in a writer's life when you ask yourself the question: do I want to be a writer? Or do I want to fling myself about in the circus of literary *braggadocio*? Do I want to strut the ring in a feathered headdress?

EDWARD. You think Vonnegut – ?

PATRICIA. I don't think of Vonnegut. I do not think of him. I do not think of him or Wolfe. (*Oh yes she does. With utter contempt*:) Vonnegut!

EDWARD. I'm very aware – I'm – Miss Highsmith –

PATRICIA. Oh no –

EDWARD. I realise that you're –

PATRICIA. Don't *fête* me! *I will not be celebrated.*

EDWARD. You and I need to have a heart to heart about the work.

PATRICIA. I don't talk about writing. *Ever*.

EDWARD. Well, I can't go home until we resolve –

PATRICIA. You can't go home?

EDWARD *reaches into his satchel and pulls out a contract, which he lays on the table with some ceremony.*

EDWARD (*determined*). Not until you sign.

> PATRICIA *watches him as he unscrews the lid of a fountain pen and lays it next to the contract. Beat.*

PATRICIA. What if I don't agree?

EDWARD. Then I guess I'm staying. (*Beat. This is the moment he's been waiting for. This is his chance to woo her with his memorised speech.*) *We have faith.* That is the bottom line. We have faith. There comes a time in every writer's life when they feel as if the fuel has dried up. They've peaked. They've written a classic or two. They've had the best seller. The invitations to literary festivals have come and gone, the fan letters, once a deluge, are now a trickle. The, the – (*Glances at the prompt notes written on his palm. With rehearsed conviction:*) insidious figure of mortality beckons on the horizon. And suddenly they feel as if they've said all they have to say. The well dries up. The words stop flowing. 'My preoccupations haunt me but where is the spark of novelty, of *originality*? Where is my capacity to surprise not just my publishers and my readers but myself. *Myself.*' All great writers experience doubt. But I am here to remind you that you do have that capacity to surprise yourself. Because life is the grist to your mill and *you still live.*

> *Beat.*

PATRICIA. *What the fuck?*

EDWARD (*failing and knowing it but still trying valiantly*). *You still live.* Oh, yes!

PATRICIA. 'The insidious figure of mortality'?

EDWARD. Well, I –

PATRICIA. Thanks for the pep talk. What I'm wondering is – Why on earth did Hunter think you would make a difference? He's a jerk and pain and a cheapskate and an asshole, but he's not a fool.

EDWARD. I persuaded Mr Hunter –

PATRICIA. I find that very hard to believe –

EDWARD. I told him I'm a Highsmith fan –

PATRICIA. Presumably you're not the only person in the company who likes my work. (*Smelling a rat.*) *Why are you here?*

Beat.

EDWARD. I'm good at what I do.

Beat.

No one likes your work more than I do.

She's not buying it. He wrestles, then confesses:

I need this.

PATRICIA. Finally!

EDWARD (*urgent*). This is the only life I want. And I'm not going to lie to you – I have to… prove myself.

PATRICIA. So they're trying to get rid of you!

EDWARD. I love publishing. I love writers. It's this or nothing.

PATRICIA. Not to denigrate it or anything, but some see publishing as a kind of well-dressed *pimping*.

EDWARD. Oh, God, no – No! It's fostering talent. It's nurturing geniuses. It's a kind of intellectual midwifery.

PATRICIA (*revolted*) Oh, Christ!

EDWARD. Literature is my whole life.

PATRICIA. Please no!

EDWARD. And it all begins with a word.

PATRICIA. *What* begins with a word?

EDWARD. The writer is alone, all alone. And she decides to make a world.

Beat. She looks at him with the first spark of interest.

She can shape it, colour it, define it, create its chemistry, its energy, its past, present, future.

He's really got her attention now. This isn't rehearsed, this is felt and she knows it.

And then, from the vapour of her exquisite imagination, she populates it. She makes her own people. What a skill that is! To make your own people! The writer wields words like the great artists once sculpted. The ghosts of the imagination whisper then grow louder, more confident – until they are indistinguishable from the real thing. (*Beat. Immaculately poised.*) The writer starts with nothing. Nothing but a word.

Beat. PATRICIA *is taken aback by his quiet eloquence. She studies him. Who is he?*

(*Breaking the spell.*) Anyway… I said – I said to Mr Hunter: I'll do anything…

PATRICIA. Really?

EDWARD. Throw anything at me.

PATRICIA. Is that so?

EDWARD. I said: What's the one job that no one in the company would do?

PATRICIA. Oh, you did?

EDWARD. Imagine, I said, if you were standing on the edge of a plunging crevasse at the bottom of which is a – a – collective noun of hungry wolves or – or – or – sharks –

PATRICIA. I get the picture –

EDWARD. And you were offered one task that would save your life if you took it and that task is so daunting, so horrific that instead, you choose to hurtle into that crevasse of sharks? *Give me that job.*

PATRICIA. I'm a shark at the bottom of a crevasse, is that it?

EDWARD (*realising too late*). Oh, no, no, no, no but after Bradley, well it was difficult to –

PATRICIA. Oh, I get it!

EDWARD. No, I mean –

PATRICIA. No one else was game enough –

EDWARD. No, but –

PATRICIA. The 'knife at the throat' thing put people off.

EDWARD. It didn't put me off!

PATRICIA. And I'm some life buoy you've thrown yourself?

EDWARD. *You have to write it.*

Long beat. He's won an admission.

PATRICIA. What if I *can't* write it?

EDWARD. You're the great Patricia Highsmith. You can write another Ripley.

PATRICIA. I'm done with Ripley.

EDWARD. I don't believe that!

PATRICIA. Don't you think I've thought long and hard about it? My most admired character? My companion? My muse? Of course I have. And I'm done with him.

EDWARD. You're *not* done with him.

PATRICIA. How the hell would you know? I'm the one who has to find him. I'm the one who draws him out, who encourages him to kill. That's *me*. *I* do that. And I'm not doing it any more.

EDWARD. You think you don't want to write a final Ripley.

PATRICIA. I *know* that I don't.

EDWARD. *I know that you do.*

PATRICIA. *Who do you think you are?*

EDWARD. All right, I'm not a famous critic or cultural commentator. But no one knows your work better than me.

PATRICIA. You couldn't have read all my work in your life span!

EDWARD. I'm young but I'm not stupid –

PATRICIA. Congratulations on that immense achievement.

EDWARD. I honestly believe –

PATRICIA. Cut the crap! Stop beating around the fucking bush! I'm not writing a Ripley so that you and your colleagues can get rich.

EDWARD. But it's not just about us.

Beat.

PATRICIA. Well?

EDWARD (*hesitant*). The fact is… You have a reputation.

Beat.

PATRICIA (*alert*). What's that supposed to mean?

EDWARD. You have a large body of work that has been… varied.

Beat.

PATRICIA. '*Varied*'?

He summons the courage:

EDWARD. Some of it is good and some of it is great. The best of it is *truly great*. But frankly… it's been a while since you've done something that *is* truly great. And…

PATRICIA *looks at him keenly.*

PATRICIA. And?

EDWARD *stares at her intensely.*

EDWARD. And not to 'beat around the fucking bush'… You're dying.

Long beat. She is shocked.

Am I wrong?

PATRICIA. That's none of your goddamn business!

EDWARD. Actually, it *is* my goddamned business. (*Beat.*) How long do you have?

PATRICIA. Not quite on my deathbed, if that is what you're looking for. But let's just say, it's freshly made up.

EDWARD. I'm sorry.

PATRICIA. Don't be sorry! I can assure you, I'm not going quietly. Death's not sneaking up on *me*. I'm not prostrating myself before it. I've earned the right to write my own death. That's *my* territory. When I go, I'm going with a *bang*, baby.

EDWARD. Okay, but you need to cement your place in the pantheon and to do that you need *one more* Ripley. Structurally tight, emotionally deft, thrilling, dark beyond our wildest nightmares: classic Highsmith.

PATRICIA. Oh, so this is all for me, is it?

EDWARD. I'm not going to lie to you –

PATRICIA. That's the second time you've said that. I think that means you *are* lying to me.

EDWARD. I would never do that! Yes, the company wants an attention-grabbing tome from the pen of a literary lioness – of course they smell an opportunity. And yes, okay, I want to keep my job. But the fact is, *you need this too*.

PATRICIA. How dare you! Stand in judgement of me, you little nothing! You're barely out of braces and you're lecturing *me* on the quality of a body of work that stretches over half a goddamn century? What would you know about 'good' and 'great'? You wouldn't recognise superior writing if it smothered you to death! Now pick up your things and get the hell out of my house! Get out before I call the cops!

He stands.

EDWARD. Miss Highsmith –

PATRICIA. *I don't like you*. And in case you think it's not personal, it *is* personal.

EDWARD. Well, you can't always judge a book by –

PATRICIA. *Oh, yes you can*. For instance, I can tell that you have an enquiring mind but a deeply inert imagination. *Edward Ridgeway*. Was there ever a more ordinary name? It's got 'boring' written all over it. You come from a *petit-bourgeois* family in Plainfield, Massachusetts, with a set of *Encyclopedia Britannicas*, only the house is gone, it's all like a dream, because your parents are dead and you're all by yourself.

EDWARD, *shocked, is silent.*

Well?

Beat. Upset, he moves towards the door, gathering his things as he goes.

Are your parents dead?

Beat. He stops and turns at the door.

EDWARD (*soberly*). Yes, they are.

PATRICIA (*with uncontained delight*). *I knew it!* Orphans – You have that awkward look of being at a party where the hosts have abandoned you and you have no one to talk to. (*Relishing the news.*) Now tell me how they died!

EDWARD. I want to talk about *you*.

PATRICIA. Of course you do. It's only natural. *I'm* fascinating. You're not.

EDWARD. I don't want to –

PATRICIA. Suicide? Drugs? Mown down by a small-town sociopath?

EDWARD. God, no!

PATRICIA. So?

EDWARD. I really would rather not –

PATRICIA. Then go!

Beat. He realises this might just save him.

EDWARD. Can I at least sit down?

PATRICIA (*relenting*). Momentarily.

EDWARD *takes his coat off again and sits down.*

EDWARD. A car wreck.

PATRICIA. I love a car wreck! (*Happy.*) Who was driving?

Beat as he summons the strength to articulate what is clearly still painful to him:

EDWARD. My father. He was a schoolteacher. Taught history. He was – (*Moved.*) He was – a wonderful man. He was – hugely loved. As a father he was – he was – I loved him.

PATRICIA. Moving right along!

EDWARD (*uncomfortable*). It was a Saturday night in spring.

PATRICIA. Go on.

EDWARD. A storm. They shouldn't have been out. There was sleet. The roads were icy.

PATRICIA. I do love an icy road! They're *lethal*!

EDWARD. Yes, ma'am.

PATRICIA. And – ?

EDWARD. The other car came from the right at an intersection and my mother took the impact.

PATRICIA. Dead?

EDWARD. Yes.

PATRICIA. Thrown outta the car?

EDWARD (*taken aback*). No, she was still in the seat.

PATRICIA. Decapitated?

EDWARD (*first time the thought has ever come up*). No – I mean… I don't –

PATRICIA. *Serious* blood and gore, obviously!

EDWARD. Can we – ?

PATRICIA. He feel guilty?

EDWARD. Ah – well – I – I was only ten. I don't really – Well, I guess so. But he was injured as well.

PATRICIA. Did he like her?

EDWARD. He was married to her!

PATRICIA. I realise that may skew the answer somewhat towards 'No' but in the spirit of open enquiry –

EDWARD. He loved her!

PATRICIA. No lovers?

EDWARD (*appalled*). Oh gosh no, no. No. They went to church!

PATRICIA. Oh, well then. Then *obviously* not. What happened to him?

The pain of the memory has not evaporated for him. He struggles to satisfy her morbid curiosity.

EDWARD. He – he died a week later. As a result of his injuries. You know, I often say to myself; at least I had them for ten years. There are people who don't get that amount of love in a lifetime. Whenever I feel self-pity, I remind myself that the size of my grief reflects the size of their love.

PATRICIA (*impatient*). Then what happened?

EDWARD. Four hundred people came to his funeral. I don't remember too much. Someone sang 'Amazing Grace'. My Aunt Verna wore a short black veil over her face. She prodded me to sit straight.

PATRICIA. Aunt Verna.

EDWARD. I didn't like Aunt Verna.

PATRICIA. Spit it out –

EDWARD. Well, she was –

PATRICIA. Oh, she was a first-class bitch.

EDWARD. Not a very nice person, no.

Beat.

PATRICIA. Who raised you?

EDWARD. My brother went to one uncle and I went to the one married to Verna.

PATRICIA. There are worse things in life than tragedy. Gives you texture… Unless it kills you, of course.

EDWARD. Well –

PATRICIA. So far this little catastrophe is the only thing *remotely* interesting about you.

EDWARD. Well, it wasn't a happy childhood after that, obviously.

PATRICIA (*pleased*). Happiness – it's overrated.

EDWARD. Even so –

PATRICIA. An opiate or a delusion. Either way it saps the *life* out of life. Anxiety, misery, these are energetic forces. *Happy people are just people who don't ask enough questions.*

EDWARD. But I –

PATRICIA. Congratulations, Mr Ridgeway. You are now qualified to make something of yourself. As you already may know, my mother made my life hell. She started by attempting to abort me with drain cleaner.

EDWARD. Jesus!

PATRICIA. My stepfather, Stanley, was an asshole but my mother was in another league – a woman with an exquisite talent for mental torture. She saved her most acute ruthlessness for me. Love was not in her repertoire – probably because she needed all the emotional space she could get for cruelty. She invested in it. She banked it. Between the two of them, those fuckers ruined my childhood.

EDWARD. Boy –

PATRICIA. I used to lie in bed at night panicked I'd die in my sleep. Childhood is just one big repository of terror in the attic of your psyche.

EDWARD. Well – I –

PATRICIA. Anything that struck terror into you as a kid is the foundation of your life. The past sits on our shoulder taunting us. Challenging us.

EDWARD. Challenging us?

PATRICIA. *To murder it.* I've been running all my life. Trying to outrun the inescapable sense that I'm doomed. (*Beat.*) We're all doomed.

EDWARD. Well, I'm not so –

PATRICIA. We're doomed!

EDWARD. I don't think I'm doomed.

PATRICIA. That's a provocative thing to say for an *orphan* without any discernable accomplishment on the horizon. Keats was *dead* by twenty-five! Emily Brontë wrote *Wuthering Heights* by twenty-nine and you're making coffee for a bunch of pansy publishers in Jew-town! That spells doom to me!

EDWARD (*irritated*). I'm sorry you don't like me.

PATRICIA. '*Like*' is overrated, too.

EDWARD. Well sorry but I like most people.

PATRICIA (*worst suspicions confirmed*). Exactly. That's *exactly* what I thought.

EDWARD. I can usually find something –

PATRICIA *and* EDWARD (*overlapping*). Something nice about anyone.

Beat.

EDWARD. Yes.

PATRICIA. I can't *stand* people who see the best. People are actually at their best when they're at their worst. *Nice* people are simply excellent narrators. They're fakes. And if you've ever met a nice writer, be warned.

EDWARD. They're not nice?

PATRICIA. *They're not a writer!* Goodbye.

He studies her and her gaze is unwavering. Reluctantly, he stands again, then spies his case, pauses.

EDWARD. What about the things that you asked for?

PATRICIA. Obviously *leave* the things I asked for.

EDWARD. Mr Hunter said you'd reimburse –

PATRICIA. Just open the bag!

EDWARD. I'll open the bag.

He takes the small case and opens it. He lifts the objects out and places them carefully on the floor in a line: three white Brooks Brothers shirts, six cans of Campbell's soups, a pair of loafers, three jars of peanut butter and twenty notebooks from Columbia University.

PATRICIA *surveys the booty carefully.*

PATRICIA. What's that?!

Long beat.

EDWARD (*tentative*). Peanut butter.

PATRICIA. Skippy.

EDWARD. It's Skippy.

PATRICIA. Skippy is *American* peanut butter. Did I write *American* peanut butter?

EDWARD. I was, well, I was in America, so I figured it would, ah, be okay to bring American peanut butter.

PATRICIA. I asked for *English* peanut butter.

EDWARD. I'm sure that wasn't in the, ah, letter.

PATRICIA. I *guarantee* you it was in the letter.

EDWARD. I don't –

PATRICIA. *It was in the letter.*

Beat.

EDWARD (*nervous*). Is it – Is it better?

PATRICIA. Fifty cents a jar cheaper! That's nothing to sneeze at.

EDWARD. No, well –

PATRICIA. Only six cans of the soup?

EDWARD. They are quite heavy. Being cans –

PATRICIA. I do apologise. I didn't realise that some Cream of Mushroom was going to cripple you.

EDWARD (*hopeful this will turn things around*). I – ah – brought you a present. Some, ah, *foie gras.*

PATRICIA (*correcting his pronunciation*). *Foie gras*. You brought me *foie gras*?

EDWARD (*slightly pleased with himself*). From *Fauchon*.

PATRICIA (*correcting his pronunciation*). *Fauchon!* Well, that's all very well but six cans of soup is a bit of a letdown! (*Beat.*) And?

EDWARD. I'm sorry. I just couldn't get it.

Beat.

I tried, I really did.

PATRICIA (*beginning quietly but in a growing fury*). You tried? You *tried*? That was the *entire* reason I agreed to see you! On account of you getting it! Get out! Fuck you, Mr Ridgeway and your *trying*. Fuck you and your pathetic lack of determination and your vast, overwhelming capacity to disappoint! Damn you! Get out! Get out! Get the fuck out of my house!

By the end of her tirade, EDWARD *has opened his backpack and drawn out a long narrow box, which he opens.*

EDWARD (*quietly, with immaculate control*). I was kidding.

She is shocked by his audacity but is immediately drawn to the object which she reverently lifts out of the box and holds up to the light. It's a black-handled, impressive, very elegant and lethal-looking knife, glinting. Her fury is suspended by the sheer charisma of the object... and a new sense of EDWARD*'s confidence.*

PATRICIA. *My God.*

Beat. Saved.

What a beauty.

EDWARD (*happy*). It really is.

She studies it with admiration that is almost sexual.

PATRICIA. A Bob Dozier fighter. Fantastically thin taper.

EDWARD. Steel mirror polish like you asked for.

PATRICIA. *Magnificent*.

EDWARD. I had to go somewhere outside Paris. It was quite a long way. To see the guy. 'It has to have the steel mirror polish,' I said. 'It's for a collection.'

No praise forthcoming. She walks over to the shelf on which is elegantly displayed a collection of weapons. Above them, on the wall, are two crossed swords, both extremely dangerous-looking, heavy and long.

PATRICIA. Those were my first pieces. Confederate swords.

EDWARD (*touching one of them*). They look... dangerous.

PATRICIA. *Don't mess with my stuff!*

EDWARD (*jumping*). Oh, absolutely!

PATRICIA. I don't like *anyone* messing with my *stuff*, Mr Ridgeway.

He is silenced. She indicates a gun mounted in a frame on the wall.

Colt. 45 double-action revolver. 1878. A dealer came through last year. *Seven hundred and fifty dollars*. This is a Bowie knife from the Civil War. Don't even ask what I paid for *that*. I feel nauseous just thinking about it. Here we have a double-barrel derringer. Beautiful, isn't it?

EDWARD. Very impressive.

PATRICIA. We revere 'art' – art – some flourish of the imagination. But what about 'engineering'? Why do we not gasp at engineering? Can engineering not be spiritually uplifting? All these weapons are as beautiful as a Van Gogh or a Modigliani, but they have beauty with a purpose. *Think* what this object of beauty can do!

EDWARD. Blow someone's head off!

She mimes the action with precision:

PATRICIA. This thoroughly beguiling, elegant piece of machinery can blow someone's head off.

EDWARD. If that's not genius, I don't know what is.

She studies him suspiciously: Is he just buttering her up?

(*Knowingly.*) Of course, if I could have anything, I'd have a US Model 1836 pistol.

Beat. Did she hear right?

PATRICIA (*carefully*). Is that so?

EDWARD. You betcha.

PATRICIA (*testing him*). Not an 1805 Harper's Ferry?

EDWARD (*perfectly aware this is his ace*). The 1836 is the most elegant flintlock martial pistol ever made, frankly.

PATRICIA (*still testing*). And after that?

EDWARD. After that, I'd take a Mauser 1893 bolt-action rifle. More reliable than the Lee–Enfield or the Mosin–Nagant. But that's just me.

Beat. She is trying hard not to show she's impressed. There is a flicker of something sexual here – his knowledge makes him sexually interesting to her and he knows it. He meets her gaze – he's playing a game here.

I guess I better call one of those very reliable cabs.

Beat.

PATRICIA (*carefully*). My instinct is telling me to throw you out on your butt. On the other hand, I made two New Year's resolutions. 'Be more tolerant' and 'Drink more'. The two, clearly, are linked.

EDWARD (*tentative*). So I can stay?

PATRICIA. The guillotine hovers.

EDWARD *is delighted. First triumph.*

What we need, as we go forward, full of no doubt *very temporary optimism*, is a beer. What do you think?

EDWARD. Well –

PATRICIA. Well?

EDWARD. It's – It's 8 a.m. –

PATRICIA. Is there a law I'm uninformed about?

EDWARD. Um – no, but –

PATRICIA. Of course it's perfectly possible there *is* a Swiss law forbidding the personal consumption of beer in your own home at 8 a.m. – because they're not generally mad *bon vivants*. No beer, no thank you, no, I'll go *jogging* and then I'll read a self-help book and eat some broccoli so that I have an excellent thirty years sitting immobile but with pumping heart in a nursing home, desperately wishing but unable to express the desire for someone to put a plastic bag over my head because I can't remember the words for plastic bag.

Beat.

EDWARD. I'll – I'll get the beer.

PATRICIA. In the refrigerator. And careful of the kitties!

He looks around and makes his way through the door to the kitchen. She waits, lovingly looking over her new weapon and checks the position of the others, finessing a millimetre here or there. She stops for a moment, listens and thinks.

(*Out loud, but to herself.*) He'd make some noise, wouldn't he?

From the kitchen, the sound of glasses on a tray.

And in all probability, break something.

From the kitchen, the sound of something smashing. She smiles.

And then he's back.

As if summoned, he enters with two glasses of beer on a tray. Self-consciously, he passes her a glass. She's savouring the beer and unafraid of silence. They sit and drink without speaking: her in control, him waiting.

So you want another Ripley?

EDWARD. Yes, we do. Because he's the greatest literary character of the second half of the twentieth century. Terrifying. Enigmatic. Human, complex and a –

PATRICIA (*soft spot*). Killer… Only thing I've created I'm
    straight out proud of.

EDWARD. You know, I –

PATRICIA (*alert*). What?

EDWARD. No –

PATRICIA. Say it!

EDWARD. Okay…Well, I think *you know* you haven't finished
    with Ripley.

Beat. She's interested despite herself.

The *great* Ripley. The *greatest* Ripley. The full-blown
    culmination of a lifetime's love affair. You've contemplated
    it, haven't you?

PATRICIA (*yes, I have*). No, I haven't.

EDWARD. You're dreaming him up right now! Of course you
    are. He's in you. When you look out at the world, you see it
    through Ripley's eyes. When you glimpse an elegant suit in
    a department-store window, you think about how that suit
    might look on Ripley, the colour of the silk tie, the way it
    sets off his eyes. I don't think you can rid yourself of Ripley.
    There's too much history. There's too much feeling.

PATRICIA *is uncharacteristically quiet.*

Come on. What's the cost of admitting it? There's no one
    here but us.

Silence.

A word, a phrase, an image…

PATRICIA *looks at him.*

PATRICIA. A newsstand in New York City.

EDWARD (*triumphant*). Thank you.

PATRICIA. A beautiful young woman is buying a newspaper.
    From across the street, Tom Ripley watches her.

EDWARD (*delighted*). Okay! Go on…

PATRICIA. Ripley follows her as she makes her way home to a large and elegant brownstone on Greene Street. There's a brass buzzer by the front door and when Ripley crosses the street after she's gone inside, he notes that it's rubbed perfectly clean of fingerprints by an assiduous maid...

EDWARD (*with almost sexual excitement*). Keep going. This is great!

PATRICIA. If I need a cheer squad I'll ask for one. (*Beat.*) The flower boxes are blooming with white tulips. Ripley can see into a parlour where the beautiful girl is smiling at an old man. There's a silver tray with martini glasses and a cocktail shaker that Ripley just knows is sterling and a small but lovely Cubist etching on the wall and a glossy black grand piano and a wall of leather-bound books. The beautiful girl sits at the piano and Ripley can hear the muted sounds of Bach's *Goldberg Variations*.

EDWARD. Fantastic!

PATRICIA. For two weeks, Ripley follows the girl. She works at a la-di-da fashion magazine, but he can tell she's the kind of girl who *wants* to work rather than *has* to. At lunchtimes, she goes to the Tick Tock Diner on 8th and 34th with other beautiful girls in well-cut clothes with straight teeth and Italian shoes and he hears them speak about a New York world he has never known: a bridal registry at Bergdorf's, martinis at The Carlyle. And so one day, Ripley brushes past her as she crosses 5th Avenue and deftly lifts her wallet from her purse. He follows her to the Tick Tock and when she goes to pay her check he says:

She indicates him. At first alarmed, he quickly comes up with it:

EDWARD. 'Excuse me, miss, but I think you may have dropped this?'

PATRICIA. And so begins his pursuit. The relentless pursuit of a girl, whose primary advantage is not her beauty, or her intellect, or her piano playing – although he likes all these things – it's her grandfather's trust fund. *Because Ripley loves beautiful things and beautiful things cost money.* Ripley is a genius when it comes to seduction.

EDWARD. No one better. He's a master.

PATRICIA. Of course, he doesn't call himself Ripley. He doesn't want anyone to make any connection with his past, so he – hmmm… let's say, he… (*The idea strikes*.) introduces himself as an orphan called – *Edward Ridgeway*.

He's thrilled by this and beams with pleasure.

At first, she resists his advances, but he has mastered the fine art of poetic strategy. He sends her a single peony –

EDWARD. Her favourite flower –

PATRICIA. – in a small box, and inside the petals is tucked an elegant diamond pin. Before too long, she allows him to make love to her. She's hooked. And then one day, she calls him, tearful, to say her grandfather has died suddenly. And the family trust is now in the hands of her great-aunt – a bitter and twisted old woman living somewhere in Europe. Not good news for Ripley. He discovers that once the old lady is gone, the trust goes to the girl. So Tom marries her, his almost-heiress. And he waits.

Beat.

EDWARD (*completely caught up*). Keep going!

PATRICIA. That's as far as I've got.

EDWARD. Oh, come on!

PATRICIA. That's it.

EDWARD (*intrigued*). What's her name?

Beat.

PATRICIA. *You tell me.*

EDWARD. What do you mean?

PATRICIA. Go right ahead!

EDWARD. But I – I –

PATRICIA. If you're so damned sure you know my style, *you* name her.

EDWARD. But I can't – I'm not –

PATRICIA. Oh dear. What a horrible shame. *Goodbye*.

EDWARD *(fast)*. Clementine Balfour.

Beat.

PATRICIA *(let's see what you got)*. All right.

EDWARD. Clementine *Harriet* Balfour.

Digging deep, gaining confidence:

Twenty-two, brunette, blue-eyed, perfect complexion, thin ankles, long neck, small waist, arched dark eyebrows, high cheekbones, a penchant for steak – rare – and she never goes anywhere without a copy of Camus in her purse.

Long beat.

PATRICIA *(impressed but grumpily)*. The Camus may be overkill.

EDWARD *(encouraged)*. Tom can see himself visiting Caravaggios in Roman churches with her and walking hand in hand into the elevator of The Ritz after an evening stroll along the Seine making summer plans for Capri… But… But… *(Building in confidence, daring himself.)* He has to get rid of the old lady. So… how? *(Beat. Triumphant.)* With a Glock.

PATRICIA. Why a Glock?

EDWARD. Because it's got a five-pound trigger-pull instead of a twelve-pound. Because it's light and reliable. Because it has no external trigger safety. And with thirty-six component parts, it has half as many as its competitors, which means fewer parts to go wrong.

PATRICIA *(momentarily stumped by his knowledge, then recovering)*. Too obvious.

EDWARD. Okay. Hiking. Pushes her off the mountain into an icy crevasse.

PATRICIA. It's been done. And she's too old to hike, for Christ's sake. Don't just throw something out there! If it's the final Ripley, we want something *elegant*… And *beautiful*… No guns. No falls.

Beat.

EDWARD. Okay. So how?

Beat.

PATRICIA. I don't know.

EDWARD. *What?*

PATRICIA. No fucking idea!

EDWARD. But you've – You've killed *thousands* of characters.

PATRICIA. *You* kill the old lady.

EDWARD. What?

PATRICIA. *You* kill the old woman. I'm busy until tomorrow.
So you can sleep on it. Let's see if you're made of sterner
stuff than 'Bradley Applebee'. (*Beat.*) And if you deliver, I'll
sign your contract.

Long beat. EDWARD *absorbs this: a momentous reprieve.
The end is in sight.*

EDWARD. A deal.

PATRICIA. I don't like noise. If I'm working I expect not to be
disturbed. You will have to amuse yourself this afternoon.
There are things are out there – *Swiss* things. Fields. Cuckoo
clocks. And by the way: it's a *pack* of wolves.

EDWARD. What about – ?

PATRICIA. Yes?

EDWARD. Well, ah, dinner.

PATRICIA. I don't eat dinner. You may forage if you wish,
like a small guest rodent. But don't open the soup cans.
They're *mine*.

EDWARD. I thought – perhaps… the – (*Careful
pronunciation.*) *foie gras*?

PATRICIA. The *foie gras*?

EDWARD. If you – I mean – You and I –

PATRICIA. *Don't touch the foie gras!* Your room is upstairs.
The bed's made up. My accountant stayed last Thursday and
I didn't change it. As far as I know, he's clean. And in the

morning… (*With genuinely creepy malevolence*.) if you make it to the morning… I expect a murder. A *good* murder. *A Highsmith murder*.

EDWARD *starts climbing the spiral staircase, then stops, suddenly captivated by a thought*.

EDWARD. You know, only you pulled it off – at least in modern times: the complete corruption of the reader.

PATRICIA. It's called good writing.

EDWARD. When he kills Dickie Greenleaf in the boat – the sheer, visceral horror of that – we identify with Ripley. We *want* him to get away with it. You smash our moral compass.

PATRICIA. Writers are exceptional because we don't care about your moral compass. We're beyond your moral compass. Moral liberty is the artist's compensation for impecunity, loneliness and unlikability. It's not my job to pass judgement – It's my job to *persuade*. The *reader* takes sides. *I* sit there, right in the middle.

EDWARD. In Switzerland.

PATRICIA. In *Switzerland*. The anatomy of a killer is always going to be more captivating than the anatomy of a victim. Because murderers *are active*. They transgress. *Transgression*… What a magnificent word. Fact is – we *all* have touches of evil.

EDWARD. We don't all commit murder.

PATRICIA. *We all might*.

EDWARD. Okay…

PATRICIA (*visceral, creepy*). I *like* murder. I've committed *thousands. With delight*. Every time I write one, I'm *plunging* in the knife, I'm *slicing*, I'm *dicing*. *I'd make a brilliant killer.*

EDWARD *is completely drawn into the vision of her murdering. Over the next section, a clear, cold chill emerges and* EDWARD *feels it viscerally*.

In every single one of us, consciously or in the realm of dreams, we contemplate the thought of taking away life.

The ultimate human power is to stop life. Take away what God made. Undo it. Who isn't interested in exercising that power? *Only liars*. Because underneath the social niceties, biding its time, is *rage*. Sometimes I wonder if it isn't the most exhilarating expression of aliveness: the act of killing.

EDWARD (*reassuring himself*). You're talking about fiction –

PATRICIA. Don't you ever ask yourself: *What would it be like?* (*Beat*.) I don't think there's a human being alive who hasn't wanted to *slay*. We hate with a passion just that bit more robust than we love. But what sorts the wheat from the chaff is... (*Looking right at him: challenging*.) *Who will act?* (*Beat*.) Who has the guts to cross that line?

Beat. EDWARD *is enthralled but appalled.*

You put two people in the same room for long enough and if you let their true selves emerge, chances are... *only one's going to make it.*

She cackles. Creeped out, he continues up the stairs.

Flickering firelight. PATRICIA *is alone in the dark. She picks up the new knife and with clear and devilish intent, climbs the stairs towards the sleeping* EDWARD.

Blackout.

ACT TWO

The next day: late afternoon.

A recording of 'Happy Talk' from South Pacific *is playing loudly on the turntable.* PATRICIA *enters, and believing she is unseen, dances with a loose, fluid pleasure, joyfully caught up in the song and singing along to the chorus.*

A more confident EDWARD *enters, unseen by* PATRICIA. *He is now wearing a dandyish suit. Above his collar is a small red cut. He watches her dance, smiling.*

PATRICIA *sights him and embarrassed, immediately stops dancing. She crosses to the record player and lifts the needle from the turntable. Long beat as they study one another. The moment breaks:*

PATRICIA (*defensive*). I happen to find show tunes uplifting.

EDWARD (*surprised*). Okay…

PATRICIA (*barking*). What?

EDWARD. Well, it's unexpected.

PATRICIA. 'Cause you know me so well!

EDWARD. Well, it's just – most writers don't –

PATRICIA. I'm not *most* writers!

EDWARD. Well –

PATRICIA. What?

EDWARD. Your most famous literary creation is a psychopathic killer.

PATRICIA. And that counts me out of the show-tunes fan club, is that it? Just because *you* don't like 'em!

EDWARD. I'm not against show tunes.

PATRICIA. You're not?

EDWARD. No-oh! I love a show tune. They're… terrific.

PATRICIA (*suspicious*). Name a show tune you like. Come on!

EDWARD. Oh, well, ah, there are so many! (*Trying to think of one*.) Many, many, many… (*Finally with relief.*) – 'Tomorrow'!

PATRICIA. 'Tomorrow'?

EDWARD. I like 'Tomorrow'.

PATRICIA. What's that from?

EDWARD. *Annie*.

PATRICIA. *Annie?*

EDWARD. The little red-headed orphan.

PATRICIA. *You Are Fucking Kidding Me*.

He's taken aback.

What about 'You're The Top' or 'Some Enchanted Evening'? What about 'Put on a Happy Face'? Good lord. *Annie*!

EDWARD (*astonished*). You *like* 'Put on a Happy Face'?

PATRICIA (*thoroughly gruff*). *Why wouldn't I?* (*Beat.*) I can see the bright side of life, for Christ's sake!

EDWARD (*over the top of her*). I'm sorry.

PATRICIA (*continuing on without irony*). – Now tell me how the old woman gets the chop. Is she brutalised? Hit over the head with an iron bar? Hog-tied? Hurled off the side of an ocean liner, slipped cyanide in her gimlet, smothered, burnt, frozen? Let's get this show on the road!

EDWARD (*deep breath*). Well…

PATRICIA. What are you *wearing*?

EDWARD (*disconcerted*). A – a suit.

PATRICIA (*indicating the cut*). And what's that?

EDWARD*'s hand reaches instinctively for the cut on his neck. Beat.*

EDWARD (*neutral*). I must have cut myself shaving.

Beat as their eyes lock.

PATRICIA. Where'd you go, this morning?

EDWARD. Walking. You were typing. And there was a snail in my bed.

PATRICIA. All part of the service.

She laughs gaily.

EDWARD. I put it back in the terrarium.

PATRICIA. Good thinking, genius.

EDWARD. What is it with the snails?

PATRICIA. I like watching them.

EDWARD. You like watching them *what*?

PATRICIA. Don't be so aggressive.

EDWARD. I'm just saying: it's not like they tap dance.

PATRICIA. I like watching them *copulate*.

EDWARD (*repelled*). Jesus!

PATRICIA. Fascinating.

EDWARD. Sorry I asked.

PATRICIA. The really interesting thing about snails is you can't tell their sex. Imagine if *they* couldn't tell. Imagine if you just didn't know if you were male or female. If your entire sense of pleasure was ambiguous.

EDWARD. Like Ripley.

PATRICIA. Like Ripley. Speaking of which –

EDWARD. I met your neighbours down the road –

PATRICIA. I didn't agree to you coming here so you could go *yodeling* in a crevasse.

EDWARD. They gave me breakfast. I only had a snack last night.

PATRICIA. You didn't help yourself to my terrarium, did you?

EDWARD. You're lucky you were out of garlic.

PATRICIA. Not funny.

EDWARD. I found a tin of beans.

PATRICIA. Jesus Christ! I was *saving* those beans for a special occasion.

EDWARD. They had 'Use by 1984' stamped on the top.

PATRICIA. They do that so suckers like you buy *more* beans.

EDWARD. Actually, I was, ah, looking for the *foie gras* –

PATRICIA. It's gone.

EDWARD. Oh!

PATRICIA. And you were right. It must have been good. Kitty *loved* it.

EDWARD *looks appalled.*

No doubt the neighbours force-fed you some disgusting strudel?

EDWARD. Delicious strudel and very nice people. They had no idea you lived here.

PATRICIA. Yeah well that's garbage. They've been trying to kill me for years.

EDWARD. He's an astrophysicist!

PATRICIA. Yeah well, he's an astrophysicist with sociopathic tendencies! They've been plotting to do away with me and it's only 'cause I'm on red alert they haven't succeeded.

EDWARD. I don't think –

PATRICIA. I didn't come to Switzerland for neighbours!

EDWARD. Why *did* you come to Switzerland?

Beat.

PATRICIA. None of your business.

EDWARD. You know, New York's changed. They've been cleaning it up. They're planning to turn the High Line into a garden –

PATRICIA (*irritated*). They want to make the old railway a garden?

EDWARD. A peaceful getaway.

PATRICIA. *Peaceful?* New York City? Jesus Christ. You want peaceful, come to Cuckoo Clock Central! Eat some Toblerone! New York City has no place being peaceful.

EDWARD. The residents – ah, seem to like the idea. Already there are wildflowers up there –

PATRICIA. The hills are alive in the Meatpacking District!

EDWARD. I think you'll notice a difference if you come back.

PATRICIA. I went back. Three years ago. I read at Rizzoli's.

EDWARD. So if you went back, then –

PATRICIA. It costs a fortune to live in New York City.

EDWARD. I live there and I'm not rich.

PATRICIA. No, but you're one big nobody. It's *cheaper* being a nonentity.

EDWARD. Is that really the reason you're here? Exiled in the Swiss Alps?

PATRICIA. What the hell is wrong with the Swiss Alps?

EDWARD. All this… neutrality. It's like… nature's equivalent of a dentist's waiting room.

PATRICIA. I don't have to endure constant interruptions!

Beat.

EDWARD (*musing*). I think it's about… status. How you're… judged.

PATRICIA. Do you think I care what a bunch of dead white American males think of my writing?

Silence.

Think it matters to me that they say I dish out potboilers because I don't happen to have a penis?

Silence.

You do know I was made an Officer of the Order of Arts and Letters of France? You do know that, don't you? Do you know what that means?

EDWARD. A grand *fromage*.

PATRICIA. A very damn grand *fromage*, baby.

EDWARD. So Norman Mailer doesn't bother you?

PATRICIA. Mailer!

EDWARD. Doesn't bother you he called you a high-class detective novelist?

PATRICIA. I know what he called me!

EDWARD. At least it was high class!

PATRICIA (*unable to contain herself, bile building*). 'Detective novels'! Was *Crime and Punishment* a detective novel? I write about *life*. Life as it *is*, no sugar added. I'm ugly at the heart, so what? *We all are*. That's what makes us more interesting than *rocks*. The French like me just the way I am. The American literary establishment? Oh, they swan about Manhattan reading the *New Yorker* but while their antecedents were building log cabins and eating corn grits, Delacroix was painting: *Liberty Guiding the People*. The French may be repulsive, but they know their stuff. Not like America where the over-praised literary fraternity – a bunch of middle-aged male writers with massive egos is fawned upon by middle-aged male *critics* with massive egos. They are locked in symbiotic, even *sexual* embrace. They *fuck each other*. There. Let's be clear. Because, apparently, women are not and cannot be geniuses.

EDWARD. I can see how that might –

PATRICIA (*on a roll*). I won't say there are days I'm not eaten up with injustice. Writers sit inside injustice very easily. It's their most comfortable chair. But I do not need to parade my insecurity by clawing my way into their good graces. *I'm a writer*. My impulses live in their own kingdom – a kingdom driven by death. And I'm rather good at writing about it. So Norman Mailer can go fuck himself. Drink?

EDWARD. Ah… Sure.

She pours two shots: one large one in a large glass for her, one small one in a shot glass for him.

Okay, so, you hate Americans. And you hate the French.

PATRICIA. Not to mention blacks –

EDWARD. You're joking, aren't you?

PATRICIA. *I'm not joking*.

EDWARD. Jesus!

Two more shots and they down them.

You're a very complicated woman.

PATRICIA. And you know so much about women! You're a homo, aren't you?

EDWARD. What?

PATRICIA. You like men.

EDWARD. That's just –

PATRICIA. You're a fairy.

EDWARD. I don't think my sexual preference is relevant here.

PATRICIA. Do you have a sexual preference? Or are you a snail?… What's the big secret?

EDWARD. It's not a secret. It's just not your –

PATRICIA. I think it's interesting you're so damn secretive –

EDWARD. I think it's interesting that a writer whose entire creative – (*Clumsy pronunciation.*) oeuvre –

PATRICIA (*correcting him*). Oeuvre. You know, with your linguistic skills, I'd stick to 'body of work'!

EDWARD (*resolving*). You know, I'm not going to let that go. You sit up here in the *Alps*, surrounded by people in *dirndls* making *fondue*, *like a fossil*. I keep thinking you know better than to be racist, but you *don't* know. 'Cause you're stuck in the 1950s when you were out there in the world and you're oblivious to the fact that *civilisation has moved on*. Ignorant views like yours have been *outed* –

PATRICIA. You're calling me ignorant – ?

EDWARD. Yes, I am!

PATRICIA. I'm not ignorant. I'm just *mean*.

EDWARD. Thanks for the newsflash! You carry on about not liking African-Americans, not realising that you're paralysed in some antiquated social bubble.

PATRICIA (*rattled*). I never said I didn't like African-Americans. I said I didn't like *blacks*. That's a much larger pool, obviously… But they shouldn't feel bad because I can't stand Jews more. And I'm not crazy about Portuguese or Latinos, either.

EDWARD. Of course you aren't.

PATRICIA. Not to mention Catholics. *Catholics!* Yuck! *Big deal. Go.* And take your contract with you!

EDWARD *looks over at the contract.*

Send Hunter my best regards! Tell him to go fuck himself! And good luck selling insurance.

EDWARD *takes a long beat and studies her carefully, reappraising.*

EDWARD (*growing confidence*). You know, I have a sneaking suspicion you say this stuff *for effect*.

She's astonished by this gumption.

PATRICIA. Oh, really!

EDWARD. All this viciousness feels a tiny bit overplayed. (*Pleased with his insight*.) I don't think you're anywhere near as awful as you come across.

PATRICIA. Believe me, I *am* this awful.

EDWARD. I don't think that these sentiments tally with your grasp of humanity.

PATRICIA. Oh, I like humanity all right, only *edited*!

EDWARD. I think you don't want to let anyone in. 'Cause you're frightened of your feelings.

PATRICIA. I *feed off* my feelings!

EDWARD. No… You *give them away*. You give them to your characters. Whatever you may be, Miss Highsmith (and let's not go there) – you are not *crude*… Your racism is *schtick*. *It's your song-and-dance act*.

Beat.

PATRICIA (*more affected than she would like to be*). I like people! Just not *all* people!

EDWARD. Who *do* you like?

PATRICIA. Plenty!

EDWARD. Who?

PATRICIA. *Lots!*

She pours them two more shots. The alcohol is beginning to work on them.

Beat.

Francis Bacon. I would have liked to have met *him*. (*On her desk.*) Here's a postcard of his *Study No. 6*. One of the screaming popes. He had a nanny that locked him in a cupboard for hours. That's why he painted in a little tiny room. Now someone your generation would be lying on the shrink's couch complaining of post-traumatic stress but Bacon said: 'That cupboard was the making of me.' *That's* an artist. Everyone else can go to hell. Especially the Jews!

EDWARD. Here she goes, *the curtain goes up*!

PATRICIA. It's a free world. If I can't stand Red Indians – and I can't, as it happens – that's my problem, not yours. You can be a one-man publicist for every two-bit minority on Earth. You can go your merry way loving everyone and everything and leave me to my exultant cynicism.

EDWARD *drowns her out with the tune and upbeat style of 'Happy Talk'.*

She stares at him: stand-off. He won the point and her confidence is surprisingly dinted. When he gains power, she loses it.

You want your goddamn contract signed?

EDWARD. You know I do.

PATRICIA (*trying to reclaim control*). *Then how did Ripley kill the old woman?*

EDWARD. Were you in my room last night?

Beat.

PATRICIA. Why?

EDWARD. Were you in my room with a knife?

PATRICIA. With a knife!

EDWARD. Were you?

PATRICIA. The return of Bradley Applebee!

EDWARD. I don't think I imagined it.

PATRICIA. What you think doesn't matter.

There's mettle in EDWARD*'s voice.*

EDWARD. The moment I walked through the door your reflex position was to belittle me.

PATRICIA. Completely unnecessary. You belittle yourself by just being you.

EDWARD. Does it occur to you that you may have got it wrong. Maybe I *am* special. You and I both know that if the past is a millstone around your neck, you either use it or kill it. You take your past and you wrap your hands around its throat and you stifle it of oxygen until it's *limp*.

She's interested in this. He knows. His confidence grows. He believes this with absolute certainty.

We embody our circumstances *and* we overcome them. What's the greatest of all human capacities? Not love. Not forgiveness. Not courage. *Transformation*. You came from *Texas* so you know that.

PATRICIA (*grudging admiration*). Huh!

EDWARD (*totally in control*). We're a nation of Jay Gatsbys. The whole point of being American is having the temerity to recast ourselves as *who we want to be*.

Taken aback at his unexpected insight and strength, she pours two more shots. They down them.

PATRICIA. Drink? Well, well... You've been hiding your light.

EDWARD. Well, you're a giant bushel.

PATRICIA. That sounds faintly obscene.

EDWARD (*new confidence*). Your mother tried to abort you with drain fluid. Your father left. You hated your stepfather, Stanley. You're a lesbian. You came of age in New York City at a time when women had to work five times harder to get half as far. You write crime – a form that no one who's anyone rates. And on top of that you've got a – *challenging* – personality. And yet you've delivered a couple of outright masterpieces.

PATRICIA. 'A *couple*'?

EDWARD. You know better than anyone the allure of transformation.

He moves closer to her. She's not displeased by his proximity.

That's *why* you wrote Ripley. Because you wanted to *be* him.

He stands very close to her. There is a distinct sexual tension. Nothing can happen but it feels like it might.

PATRICIA. Elementary school. In Astoria. One morning when I was about ten, Miss Pembroke asked me to open the window. I had to shimmy up a pole and I looked out and there was the day. I saw a man, just an ordinary hatless man in an inexpensive suit, with a crisp white shirt and a tie, probably a salesman, walking down the pavement, carrying a neat brown briefcase. A pretty girl passes him and he nods. Something happened to me when I saw that man. I've never forgotten his face or the sensation I felt. The deepest, purest envy. All my life I've been chasing that man... What are you chasing?

EDWARD. I think you know.

Beat.

PATRICIA. You've got very cocky all of a sudden.

EDWARD. Think I'm scared of you?

PATRICIA. If you're smart, then you should be. (*Very creepy.*) Has it occurred to you… *Maybe you won't get out of here alive?*

He bends down behind her sitting in the chair. He leans in, close to her ear from behind. With distinctly sexual overtones:

EDWARD. That excites me more than it worries me.

She smiles, looking out, feeling his breath on her neck.

PATRICIA (*lost in his words*). Again.

EDWARD. It excites me.

PATRICIA. Again.

EDWARD. *You* excite me.

Beat. Something complicit and intense in the silence. She breaks the moment by pouring two more shots. They down them.

(*Very confident.*) Tom Ripley tracks down the old woman in Europe – He tells her he's been sent – by the bank—as a courtesy to make sure she's happy with the way the trust has been handled. He spills his drink and dashes to the kitchen to grab a cloth and swiftly, neatly, unlatches the window and pockets a shopping list written by the housekeeper. He finds out that every Wednesday, the old woman plays bridge in town and the housekeeper has the evening off and stays out of town.

PATRICIA. Okay, so – ?

EDWARD. The next Wednesday, Tom climbs in the window and cleans the apartment: top to bottom, every surface, meticulous, leaving a note he has perfectly forged in the housekeeper's hand, to say she took the opportunity to spring-clean. The next morning, the old woman wakes up dead.

PATRICIA (*pleased*). Carbon tetrachloride. Carpet cleaner. Toxic.

Over the next speech, EDWARD *takes a cigarette from* PATRICIA*'s packet, lights it and inhales as he describes Ripley's similar actions.*

EDWARD. Tom climbs in the window again, makes sure she's tucked up in bed as if she's just had a heart attack in her sleep. He destroys the forged note from the housekeeper and then he can't resist a moment of self-congratulation. He takes a cigarette from the old lady's packet, lights it, and takes a deep intake of nicotine and – (*His eyes alight on* PATRICIA*'s record player.*) and he puts a record on.

He quietly sings a couple of lines of 'Happy Talk'.

Beat.

(*Waiting.*) Well? You've got to admit. It's good.

Beat. She pours them both another shot. They both down it. They regard each other warily. She picks up the pen and her hand hovers over the page. Beat. She signs and passes him the contract.

PATRICIA. Tell Hunter he'll get his book.

He studies her.

EDWARD. What happens now?

PATRICIA. Well, wouldn't you like to know?

EDWARD. Is that the end?

PATRICIA. Of course that's not the end. That's just the beginning.

EDWARD. Tom goes on to kill again?

PATRICIA. You know he does.

Beat. This conversation marks new possibility. He gets up and walks towards the spiral staircase. He now speaks with a burgeoning air of control.

EDWARD. All right, so this is what I'm going to do. I'm not going to leave in the morning. I'm going to check my bed for snails. And then I'm going to sleep. And tomorrow, I'll help you make *this* Ripley as good as the 'talented'.

He starts walking up the stairs, as if to bed. Suddenly he stops, as if he's just had a thought.

Where does the old woman live?

PATRICIA. *Switzerland!*

EDWARD *pauses a moment to take this in, then resumes climbing the stairs, until he disappears.*

Blackout.

ACT THREE

Early morning. EDWARD *enters, looks around: no* PATRICIA.
*He is very nattily dressed: a shirt, well-tailored pants, and a
cravat. He wanders over to* PATRICIA*'s desk, looking it over
and moving things an inch or two, rearranging. He lights one of
her cigarettes and picks up one of her notebooks and flicks
through it. Catching a glimpse of the contract still lying on the
table where she signed it, he picks it up and with a lighter, sets
it on fire, dropping it into the waste-paper bin. As it flares and
then flickers and goes out, the phone rings. He stares at the
phone and then looks to see if* PATRICIA *is coming. After a
couple of rings, he lifts the receiver.*

EDWARD (*scrupulously polite and confident*). Hello?… Yes, it
is… I'm afraid she's not here at the moment, this is her
assistant. May I take a message?… Oh, well, no, I'm afraid
that Ms Highsmith is out of the country. Are you calling
from the United States?… Okay… From her publishing
company?… Edward… Uh-huh… Edward… *Ridgeway*?…
(*Without writing it but as if he is*.) Can you spell that?… Uh-
huh… Uh-huh… Uh-huh… (*Repeating*.) Assistant to Mr
Hunter?… I've got that… Oh, you will? Arriving in Tegna
next Thursday… Well you can go fuck yourself,
motherfucker! I was not put on this planet to answer the
telephone to pathetic little publishing hacks like you, sitting
in your tiny windowless office in the middle of Manhattan
dreaming about the life you might have had if you had even
one ounce of my fucking talent… *je ne viendrais pas te
chercher si tu rôtissais en Enfer*.

Towards the end of EDWARD*'s phone call,* PATRICIA
*enters carrying a breakfast tray, laden with eggs, coffee,
cutlery, napkin and salt and pepper. Overhearing his
viciousness, she backs out of the room so that he doesn't see
her. After he hangs up the phone, she re-enters.* EDWARD
suddenly notices her, uncertain if she's heard anything.

Their eyes meet. Long beat.

PATRICIA. I went to a great deal of trouble making you breakfast.

EDWARD. I'm touched.

PATRICIA. Are you hungry?

EDWARD. I'm *ravenous*.

> EDWARD *sits and spreads the napkin on his lap.* PATRICIA *sits opposite him.*

(*Surprise.*) They actually look quite good.

PATRICIA. I do something, I do it properly.

> *She's priming herself for another round. Over the course of* PATRICIA*'s speech,* EDWARD *readies himself to eat, having buttered his toast, applied salt and pepper, etc., but as she reaches the second half and he is ready to take his first mouthful, his appetite starts to wane. She gradually re-embodies her confidence:*

You know, it's not murder that interests me. It's *love*. Love is what interests me. It's just that love is indivisible from murder. I like guns. And knives. I like strangling and drowning. I like the wax museum attendant who kills his customers and turns them into wax sculptures. I dream of beheadings. And I *love* poison. (*Beat.*) I *especially* love poison. (*Beat.*) Because poison is so playful. One droplet of dimethyl mercury can penetrate cell membranes and… devour the brain cells like termites.

> *Beat.* EDWARD*'s fork, laden with food, is poised in his hand, paralysed in mid-air.*

Snake venom. Simply *marvellous*.

> *She leaves long enough a beat to make him think she's finished. He moves the mouthful towards his mouth and she starts up again and he stops again.*

Not to mention, the classics. Arsenic – unoriginal but with a certain iconic status – a little will make the victim weak and confused, then low blood pressure, nausea, vomiting, paralysis and the really great thing about it, the *fabulous* thing about it, that makes it the poison of choice for murderers everywhere and for always, is that it has no colour. (*Beat*.) And no smell. (*Beat*.) And no taste.

She looks at him: challenging, her control back. Long beat. Slowly he moves the fork to his mouth and with great deliberation eats the mouthful. She watches for a few moments. Suddenly, PATRICIA *notices the objects on her desk have been moved.*

(*Calmly*.) Did you move my things?

EDWARD (*not a care in the world*). Oh. I guess I did.

PATRICIA. *You moved my things?*

EDWARD. I do apologise, Pat, but honest to God, I do think it's time you lightened up about that stuff.

PATRICIA (*quietly*). I beg your pardon?

EDWARD. It's not as if they're Fabergé eggs! It's just a bunch of mementos.

PATRICIA (*growing fury*). How dare you speak to me like that!

EDWARD. I *said*: I apologise.

PATRICIA. Get the fuck out!

EDWARD. I can't do that, Pat.

PATRICIA. You *can* do it if I *make* you do it.

EDWARD. That wasn't the deal.

PATRICIA. You'll do exactly what I tell you to! If I want you to leave, you'll leave.

EDWARD (*softly*). But that's *not* what you want.

PATRICIA. I can snap my fingers any time I like and you'll vanish right out that door in a puff of goddamn smoke.

EDWARD (*very calm, assured*). Then snap your fingers.

Beat as they both acknowledge that she will never do that.

PATRICIA. Who was on the phone?

EDWARD◻TOM (*very casual*). Edward Ridgeway. From New York.

PATRICIA. The *actual* Mr Ridgeway?

TOM. The *actual* Mr Ridgeway.

Beat.

PATRICIA. Whatcha do, Tom? Cut the brake cable?

Long beat. Through the following speech, EDWARD *slowly morphs into* TOM. *Lighting helps to physically transform him. The overall effect is bone-chilling as the psychopathic* TOM *emerges.*

TOM. I waited for spring, I knew from my paper round that spring rains make the roads greasier. I saw some fierce smashes on Middleton Road, with the bends and the river flooding: Saturday nights on newly wet roads, people hurrying to parties, running late. They were driving to bridge. Saturday night. Dad had already had a couple of drinks. Going to the Fidgetts' up on Hastings Road. I was home with my brother. When they left, I hugged them both and in that final embrace I already felt a kind of… release. I watched TV and sat there waiting for the knock on the door. I thought: *Get ready, Tom. You're going to have to fake it.* (*Beat.*) But from the moment the knock sounded, and I opened the door to the policemen, I was right there, right inside my own performance. I could hear myself – exquisite, subtle — a model of innocence. *We've got some bad news kids and I think you need to sit down. Is there a grandma we could call? Or an aunt? That's it,* I thought, *this is exactly how it played out in my imagination.* He's doing it *the exact same way*! The miracle of it! *'Is there a grandma we could call? Or an aunt?'* One of the cops was tearing up – I knew this would go down as an anecdote about the difficulty of a policeman's job — To tell a couple of kids – just like his own boys – that their lives were forever altered. And all the time I was standing there thinking: *it's not that hard. It's actually not that hard to kill.*

PATRICIA *absorbs the unambiguous arrival of* TOM RIPLEY.

PATRICIA. *What would happen*, you thought to yourself, *if I was alone in the world*? What could I do if there was no one to hold me back, to remind me I'm nothing special?

If there was nothing to name me, categorise me, fix me in space and time... *Who might I be?*

TOM. Who I wanted to be.

PATRICIA. Who *I* wanted you to be. I've been waiting –

TOM. I know.

PATRICIA. I've been waiting so long —

TOM. *For your talented Mr Ripley to come back.*

Beat.

(*Utterly assured.*) I'm the only one who knows all of you.

She's vulnerable and silenced by the truth.

Isn't that right? Poor Pat... You left your country because it fucked you up and then hung you out to dry. You don't like Europe but you'd rather be a somebody somewhere you hate than a nobody somewhere you belong. Your lovers were difficult and cruel because cruel women are the kind of women you like. You've ended up in a Swiss bunker with some cats and a couple of hundred snails. You're scared you're going to be judged for your worst work, not your best. You wake up every morning to the relentless obsessive prison of acquired objects and your blank page and you drink yourself through the day until lo and behold, the next day turns up. It's an existence, but was it a *life?*

From this point, PATRICIA*'s power has evaporated and she is newly vulnerable. She knows the end is coming.*

PATRICIA. A writer doesn't have to like their life. In fact, it's better if they rail against it.

TOM. Words turned you into *God*. And all these years you couldn't go 'out there' into the real world because you didn't *write* it. Things happen unbidden. People don't behave the way you want them to. *And you don't like it.*

PATRICIA. That's right, I don't. Look around me: everything has its place. Right where I put it. Just like the words. Why have I spent so much time finding the perfect location for things? Because just outside the door, *chaos lies in wait.*

Beat. He moves towards her.

TOM. I'm going to last a lot longer than you will.

PATRICIA. You exist because of me!

TOM. Or is it the other way around? I love you, Pat. And you love me too, don't you?

PATRICIA. Of course I do. There is only one enduring love affair in a writer's life: the love affair between the intensity of what I feel and how it woos my typing hand. *That* is love.

TOM. You can say it, Pat. You can say it, you know.

Beat.

PATRICIA (*this is hard for her. She's never said it, but it's been the fundamental truth of her life and now is the time to speak it aloud*). I need you.

TOM *and* PATRICIA *draw closer. They look intensely at each other. They kiss on the mouth, but it's love, not passion – the end of something, not the start of it. They break off. That kiss has meant something very profound to her.*

TOM (*tenderly*). It's been fun.

PATRICIA. We were good.

TOM. We were *great*.

PATRICIA. So it wasn't carbon tetrachloride?

TOM. We *both* know... I used a Bob Dozier fighter with a fantastically thin taper and a steel mirror polish.

She picks up the knife reverently and deftly runs her finger along the blade. Eyes lock. She moves towards him, holding the knife, her intention ambiguous. She looks as if she's going to kill him but instead, she slips the knife into his hand.

PATRICIA. Now, wasn't that a perfect choice?

She walks over to the window and pulls aside the curtain. In her mind's eye, the Swiss mountain view dissembles and fades into a different view: New York around 1931.

TOM, *holding the knife, watches her.*

Where have the mountains gone?

TOM. What do you see?

PATRICIA. It's a sidewalk. And some shopfronts. My feet are hitting the ground in a quick rhythm. I'm hurrying to my meeting. My trench coat is open and under it, I've a suit on and a crisp white shirt and a tie and I'm carrying a neat brown briefcase. I've left my hat at home and the breeze is riffling through my short hair. I pass a pretty girl and I nod but I need to hurry. I need to hurry but it's okay, it's all okay… I'm on my way.

A moment between them: caught in time and light. A moment of absolute mutual understanding.

TOM stabs her: a violent, clean thrust. She collapses. He watches her a moment, then lays her out carefully on the sofa. He lights a cigarette from PATRICIA*'s packet and takes a deep intake of nicotine. He walks to the record player, shuffles through the records and puts on 'Happy Talk'. As it plays, he looks over to her desk, walks to it, sits in her chair, straightens up and begins to type as the lights fade to black.*

The End.